To Marian Quigley
who also called
it home —

Virgil Kherdian.

Sebastopol
May 5, 1998

Books in David Kherdian's *Root River Cycle*

Homage to Adana
I Remember Root River
Place of Birth
Root River Run
A Song for Uncle Harry
The Dividing River/The Meeting Shore
Friends: A Memoir
Asking the River
My Racine
I Called It Home

I CALLED IT HOME

By David Kherdian

BLUE CRANE BOOKS
WATERTOWN, MASSACHUSETTS

I CALLED IT HOME
By David Kherdian

First Published in 1997 by
Blue Crane Books
P.O.Box 291, Cambridge, MA 02238

First Edition
1   3   5   7   9   10   8   6   4   2

Racine map and cover drawing of Island Park by Nonny Hogrogian
Book design, typography & electronic pagination by
Arrow Graphics, Inc. Watertown, Massachusetts
Printed in Canada

Library of Congress Cataloging-in-Publication Data
I called it home / David Kherdian.
p.   cm.
ISBN 1-886434-07-7 (alk. paper)
1. Kherdian, David—Childhood and youth.
2. Armenian Americans—Wisconsin—Racine—Biography.
3. Racine (Wis.)—Social life and customs.
4. Young men—Wisconsin—Racine—Biography.
5. Boys—Wisconsin—Racine—Biography.
I. Title.
PS3561.H4Z472   1997
811'.54   97--16009
[B]—dc21   CIP

Grateful acknowledgment is made to the *Journal Times* (Racine, Wisconsin) for first publishing many of these chapters serially, with period photographs, and to *Ararat* magazine, where a number of chapters were presented as a cover feature, with drawings from old photos by Nonny Hogrogian.

In addition, *Shambhala Sun, Wisconsin Academy Review, Impressions,* and *Forkroads,* each published single chapters, as did the anthology

GETTING BY: STORIES OF WORKING LIVES

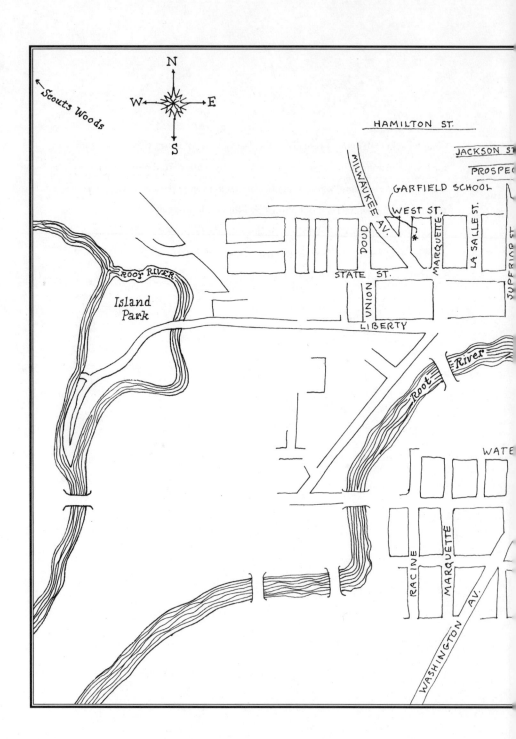

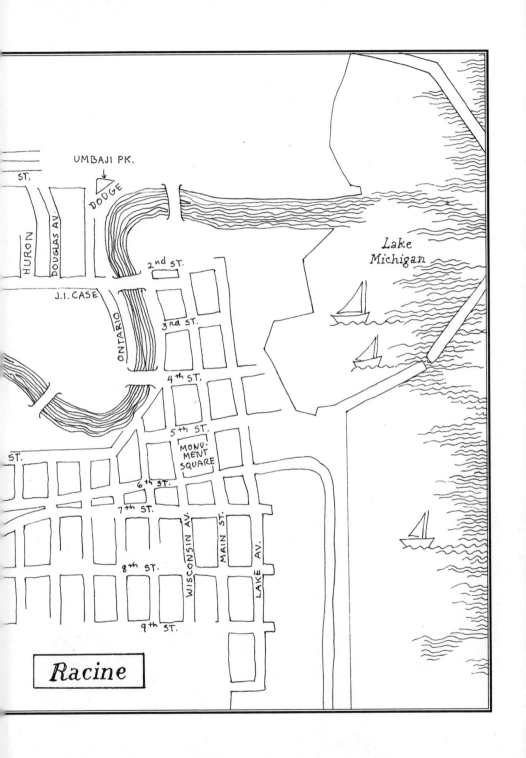

UMBAJI PK.

ST.

DODGE

HURON
DOUGLAS AV.

Lake
Michigan

2nd ST.

J.I. CASE

ONTARIO

3rd ST.

4th ST.

5th ST.

ST.

MONU-
MENT
SQUARE

6th ST.

7th ST.

WISCONSIN AV.

MAIN ST.

LAKE AV.

8th ST.

9th ST.

Racine

I CALLED IT HOME

RACINE, WISCONSIN

I t was an odd place to be born into.
What were we doing here, and how did it happen
that we, the Armenians, had found this place?

Or had it found us? Or was it lost and we in it—
as it always seemed to me. A city without a purpose,
and we abiding in it.

It was said in those days that the business of
America was business. The lore of factories, foundries,
machine shops, garages, etc., was not the lore of business, although it *was* business, no doubt, that was
behind their reason for being.

The businessmen had come to the docks in New
York to hire the emigrants off the boats. This is how it
started.

The first Armenians moved to Racine around the
turn of the century. Racine had already passed out of its
wagon making era, and was now producing farm
machinery. The wagons belonged to the era of western
expansion, and the implement industry to its settle-
ment and exploration.

The businessmen were there for the money—big
money. The workers were also there for the money—
enough to survive on. But the work itself, the machinery itself, the result and fulfillment of the production of
it itself . . . well, to put it simply, it was a means to an
end—and the end again was money: money enough
for the rich, and money enough for the poor.

So the meaning of the city, as well as the communities within it, that were formed by the numerous sub-cultural pockets: Danes, Scotch, Irish, Welsh, English, Norwegians, Poles, Czechs, Bohemians, African Americans, and, to a lesser extent, Jews, Greeks, Italians and Armenians, did not lie in the goods produced, but from what could be salvaged from the wreckage of labor, whose only meaning was survival—survival with whatever dignity and pride were possible.

This was the shaky foundation on which the city was built, and its purpose was to serve the needs of a growing, hungry nation. Within this drama, the real drama of life would be enacted.

Armenian Town consisted of the streets running off State Street, beginning at the depot and running east to Root River, one block short of Main Street, where State Street would end. The streets were, west to east, Garfield, Peck, Wilson, Silver, Doud, Union, Milwaukee Avenue, Marquette, La Salle, Superior, Huron, Douglas Avenue, and Erie. It would also include that portion of Liberty Street paralleling State Street—from Marquette to the depot—and of course State Street itself, which was largely commercial, with only a few buildings given over to apartments and boarding houses.

At the lower end of State Street, between Huron and Douglas Avenue, was the J. I. Case plant, the city's principal factory, where the majority of the Armenians worked.

943 SUPERIOR STREET

My mother and father had moved from 943 Superior Street to 1010 Superior Street two years before I was born.

We lived in that house until 1958, when my father died.

The other house, the one my parents thought of as their first home, even though they were renting— for they had previously lived first in an adjoining apartment alongside relatives, and then in a tiny three room apartment behind a barber shop—was the home in which they intended to begin their family.

But it was not to be.

Perhaps it was my mother's nesting instincts, because she did not conceive until she had safely moved into her own home.

I walked by 943 Superior Street every day of my life. It meant nothing to me, even though I knew it had once been the home of my parents. Not until my last year in grade school, when a family rented it whose son was a school chum of mine, did I visit that house for the very first time.

I was a child, my parents were strangers, what could a home, any home, mean to me?

My parents had placed a root there, but I had not as yet placed a root anywhere—and it was only after I had placed many roots of my own that I began to see the necessity of going back and unearthing and examining some of the roots that I and they had earlier put down.

My parents were living in the diaspora, having fled their homeland, Turkey (because it was not Armenia, they spoke of it always as the homeland, never as Turkey), and so they had a deep need, based on fear and insecurity, to move as little as possible, and to live (as much as possible) an undisturbed and secure life. Although I inherited many things from them: fear of starvation and persecution, as well as the feeling that I, too, was living in exile (and was therefore homeless), I did not have a need for the security that seemed, from my child's point of view, to be the compelling force or motivation in their lives.

Later, I came to understand that all of ordinary life is conditioned by fear, and that, in fact, we are all of us exiles, having come we know not from where, and bound we do not know to what place.

THE CHILD

The child's world is numerous, but the place of his birth is the only place there is. Far away places do not figure in the life of his imagination, for the other side of the city is already beyond his compass and comprehension. Not only would he be lost if he were suddenly there, he has no reason to want to be there. Where he is is where he needs to be—at least at the start.

Thrown into the pool of life, we follow the concentric circles out, little by little, and each of us stops at a different place, with some of us never able to stop, until, having circled the globe, we return to our one spot and look at it all again, carefully, within the perspective now of time, and wonder again what it was that brought us here, and what it was that brought us back.

NAMES

My first nickname occurred at the same time, almost to the day, of my given name. I was born weighing 5 lbs, 4 oz. Because of my small size I was called Peanut, and it was said—by our neighbor, Clara Zaehler—that I could fit into a shoe box. There was something so final about the telling of this story, that when I was old enough to hear it myself, I actually believed that I had been placed into a shoe box upon my arrival home from the hospital. I used to wonder what it must have felt like.

I never did learn my head to toe measurement.

Although I arrived just before the close of 1931, I was in plenty of time for the Depression. I was grateful for the era or period I was born into, for I survived it without even knowing I had done so, or that doing so was something of an accomplishment.

1931.

1 is the opening and closing digit, with the next number 9, being divisible three times by the 3 that follows it.

Much better than 1932.

I figured I must have been lucky. I had arrived small, but in the nick of time.

ENGLISH

I never felt at home in Racine.

Not as an Armenian, and not as an American— although of course I did not know for a very long time that I *was* an American, or even that this earth, this place of my birth, *was* America.

My parents decided that I could not go on playing with the neighborhood children when the only language I knew was Armenian, and the only language they knew was English.

They enrolled me in the nursery school at Central Association on Wilson Street.

I was four years old.

I still have two nursery school remembrances: taking a nap, and drinking milk. The only other memory I have of that experience is hiding under the bed when the truant officer came to fetch me during my first week of school.

There we were, the three of us, in my parent's bedroom: the truant officer, my mother, and me— under the bed.

"He not here," I can remember my mother saying. "I can't imagine it where he is."

I admired my mother for that simple act of courage and good sense. I knew then, at the age of four, that this stranger, who was my mother, was perhaps not a complete stranger after all, and with one swift act, I accepted her, more or less totally, into my life.

THE BRIDGES

O urs was a city of parks and bridges. Tiny parks, short bridges, with each representing a span in fact and in time.

Crossing the State Street bridge for the first time, holding onto my mother's hand, I looked down and saw the brown, murky water. I was enthralled and amazed. I had never seen moving, living water before.

After we crossed the bridge it lifted its mighty weight, and we watched as a coal barge pushed its load from the right hand of our world to its left. Right was Lake Michigan, that we could smell and almost see in the distance, and left was the winding river as it turned the bend and disappeared, taking the coal barge mysteriously out of sight.

The gas bubbles I had been watching, I took to be the life of water, the life within the water. Fish? Minnows? I do not know what I thought or believed.

We stood for a moment or two in silence and then resumed our walk. I must have been four years old.

THE BRIDGE

The State Street bridge would be my bridge for many years to come. It was the bridge I would cross most often, on my way to the Mainstreet Theatre and the movie houses beyond: Badger, Venetian, Rialto, as well as the pool hall below Ace Grill, the pinball machines at the Arcade, Luby's Bowling Alley, where I later set pins, and of course for shopping, especially in the fall, before the start of the new school year.

Later there would be other bridges.

At the bottom of Liberty Street, the Island Park bridge, as well as the one at the end of Sixth Street, its other entrance—that I only discovered years later. Another, the Main Street bridge, could almost be seen from the State Street bridge, and was the last Root River bridge before the river emptied into the lake.

These were the main bridges—the city bridges—the ones I would have to cross and recross as I went out from home and began to experience the life of the city.

I would later discover other bridges, in the city and out of the city, as I moved through my days, following the life of people and the life of water. One took me to the outer events that nourished my thirst for the meaning of life, and the other, the life of water, brought me to inner events, and carried me to deeper and deeper streams within myself.

The bridges I traveled over carried me to both.

THE CITY OF MAN

Our city is unlike any other.
The others are either all alike, with variations both difficult to discern and easy to forget, or, if they are unusual, our experience of them is partial. But the city that holds us from our first breath of life is complete in its understanding of us, if we are incomplete in our understanding of it.

It made us, and we cannot unmake it.

Its treasure for us is its fullness, for it is the one complete experience we have. For once we traversed it, one step at a time, slowly, measuring each carefully taken step: watching and waiting.

The lore of a city is in its streets, beginning first with one's own, and then moving outward to the others.

It was on Superior Street one night that I first learned that God was not Armenian, and it gave me my first taste of identification, and that terrible sense of the world that is not I.

That night I incorporated the Armenian nation into my "I," perhaps to make myself less solitary, less vulnerable and less alone.

A bunch of us boys between the ages of six and eight, were gathered on the curb. Mikey Kaiserlian, Dickie Steberl, Junior Rognerud, and three or four others, whose names are lost to memory. I believe I was the youngest. God was mentioned, and then at once given a nationality.

Someone said he didn't have a nationality. Another said God was American. And then all at once I knew, or thought I knew—God was Armenian.

If I was the son of God, and surely I was, and if I was Armenian, then God was Armenian. I was adamant at first, and then I fell silent, partially because I was being contradicted, but really because I felt certain, and needed neither to convince myself, nor could I be argued out of my conviction.

Looking up at the stars, I knew my rightful home, my rightful father, my true identity. Since that day I have never really been convinced of anything made by man or believed by man.

Once before, that same blue bowl of heaven cracked and shattered over the lives it sheltered—and my mother, her family and her nation were put on the road to death. They had been secure in their religion, and their God—they felt—had failed them. Had He, or had man failed God—again! Was I disillusioned with my friends, or was I disillusioned in myself?

ESSENCE

My quarrel with life was deep and endless.

Did it begin on that night when I was unable to believe that God was not Armenian? I don't think so, although that is my first remembrance of feeling separate and cut-off—even though I did not know then what I felt cut-off from. Was it God? Was it my friends? Or was it my first experience in feeling—really knowing—that I was in exile from my true home, that I began to feel was denied me because I was Armenian. And yet it was as an Armenian that I was trying to make my return.

I was confused and lost, and I did not know which way to turn.

It would be many, many years before I would have a question that would touch me as deeply as that question did. And it would be even longer before I would value not knowing as a thing in itself. For it is only from not knowing, from feeling cut-off and abandoned that something new can enter and begin to be formed deep inside of us, where essence waits to grow.

THE FATHER

Does everyone think their mother is special? Are all sons ashamed of their fathers? Obviously not. But because it was overwhelmingly true for me for most of my childhood, I took it to be something more than the condition of my life.

Naturally, it was my father I defended. It was with him that I felt identified, and not only because we shared the same sex, but because he was vulnerable, on the edge, and—it seemed to me—fighting daily for his life.

My mother seemed always to be in control of herself, and in charge of the marriage and the home. My father was not. Nor was I.

CHESTNUTS

O f all the trees, of all the treasures that grew above the ground, the bounty, the prize, the endless treasure, was chestnuts.

We would watch from the ground all summer long, staring up at their green, spiked and forbidding husks. Between late summer and early autumn, when the school doors opened, their husks began to turn color, the first stage of fruition, as they prepared to fall to the earth, split open and reveal their food—that we never though of as food, but rather as an emblem of something—we knew not what.

We did not always wait for them to fall— although later in the season, we would kick among the dead leaves, startled (always hoping to be startled), as we came upon an opened husk, that revealed a portion of the brown and shining treasure inside.

But long before this we would attack the tree, climbing from branch to branch, filling our shirts, and spilling what we could not contain onto the ground.

I still remember my first chestnut autumn, when a bunch of us boys converged on the tree at 957 La Salle Street, and forgot all time and arrived at the school door long after the final bell rang.

Five tardy youngsters, sweating, yearning, abashed.

THE BINS

Playing by night was not the same as playing by day. The games were different, and different still the moods and the sounds.

My solitary flight had ended—for all day I would be alone on Root River, or, occasionally, Lake Michigan. After supper, and after dark had set in, I would leave the house to play with the gang, who converged from the neighboring streets, as well as from our own: La Salle, Jackson, Prospect, and Superior—always a good block to play on because of the abandoned factory across the street from my house, where hardly a window remained to be broken, and the woodwork factory it joined, with its flat, easy-to-climb roof (but with low hanging wires that left both Jerry Hansen and me with permanent scars on our foreheads), and its bins, where the remains of paint and lacquer cans and chemicals were dumped or discarded. The three bins, which bordered the factory, were cement-walled and partitioned, and ran perhaps halfway down the length of Superior Street at its dead end.

These bins, perhaps as self-protection, were sealed off by an easy-to-climb red wooden fence. I have given all this an elaborate description because it was here, gagging on the mixed metallic and acidic stink of the refuse in the bins, that I inhaled my first cigarette. I took a sudden jolt. It felt like the kick of a mule, but with this difference: the mule was inside of me and trying to get out. It was a strange experience, unprepared for, unexpected, a ritual practiced by all the youth of my generation, but not commonplace on that account or for that reason.

Later, we smoked in the back seat of the Model A parked in Zaehler's back yard. It must have been a junker. It was parked not fifty yards from the back of my house. I had this certain sense that my mother knew (but chose not to reveal that she knew) that I was out there with one of my buddies, secretly smoking up a storm.

THE COIN BARONS

The Public Fruit Market was situated on the corner of State and Superior Streets. On the Superior Street side of the market there was a metal grating between a portion of the sidewalk and a ground floor window. It extended approximately two feet from the window, and the boxed hole was probably two or three feet deep. Its true depth was difficult to gauge because it was packed with all manner of refuse: papers, leaves, wrappers, onionskins, etc., all of them in various stages of decomposition, piled layer upon layer.

Each time I looked into the hole it was a little different, and therefore more or less new. This in itself was interesting.

But the thing about it that was most interesting of all, was that from time to time there would be a coin or two hiding among the wrappers and leaves.

We would stare down each time we walked by, and every now and then there it would be: a penny or a nickel, and sometimes even a quarter or a dime, staring at us, tempting us.

The appearance of the money had something to do with the constant stream of traffic passing through the open doors of the market.

The grating was just far enough away from the Superior Street entrance to keep our own comings and goings free of the piercing eyes and unholy wrath of the bad-tempered Jew who owned and ran the market.

We had an idea, and the idea was this: we would

tie a used piece of juicy bubble gum onto a length of string and witch one of the coins—or *all* of the coins—out of the hole, past the metal grating and into our hands.

This is how the dream of free money was entertained among the Superior Street hoodlums aged six and seven. The idea of our little plan and the thrill that went with it penetrated deep into our greedy little marrows.

I cannot remember now if we even once tried out our little scheme, or, if we did, if our success was to the tune of one cent, two cents, or five. Had it been to the tune of a quarter, I'm sure it would not have been forgotten.

Perhaps it was enough that we dreamed it.

My logical mind tells me now that a coin will not stick to a piece of bubble gum.

Fortunately, I did not have a logical mind then, nor even much of an unlogical mind. What I had—what all of us had—was pure imagination, which was constantly and easily bent in the direction of intrigue, mystery and suspense.

And lore—any lore! But in this particular case the lore of free money, that was there to be had if one was clever enough, and could artfully lower down tied-on bubble gum through a grate, past all the items it wanted to stick to, and then, at last, drop it *precisely* on the desired coin. And then, working it inch by inch upward, and at last, miraculously up through the iron grating and into the safety of the other hand—and then, quickly into our safety deposit pockets.

Ah, what triumph! Ah, just look at the Superior Street Big Shot, strutting up the block with the captured coin in his pocket! Ah, the glory of the clever heist!

I'm sure it never happened once.

THE BOTTLES

We liked breaking bottles. We neither thought of it as destructive, nor did we value the empty bottles we broke. The thrown stone or hurled bottle, the explosion or shattering, this is what attracted us to the game. This is what we valued.

Best of all was the quick pop sound of exploding light bulbs. Their destruction was total. One instant a light bulb, whole, with a little tinny rattle (along with the telltale black smudge on top), and then pouff—nothing! Only the tin base and the dangling guts, squirming onto the ground.

Perhaps it was that we liked putting things to an end. A clean death, swift, instantaneous and total.

Sometimes one of us would throw a light bulb into the air, while the other flung a stone. The thrower would have one, or at best two chances to hit the ascending, descending bulb before it exploded on the ground.

This was not the preferred ending.

If we couldn't hit them in midair, it was better to hurl them against a brick wall, which was the fate reserved for all the other bottles, although there were other days when we lined them atop a fence and hurled rocks as hard and as fast as we could. No turns, no protocol, no victory or defeat. Just smash, smash, smash.

And then one day a shard flew back at me and took a bite out of my right index finger, leaving a thick one-inch scar that is staring at me now as I write. A funny companion of days gone by. A memoir of lost time. A message that taught me that outer acts of violence inevitably return to their source.

FARMERS, MARKETS, MADMEN

Before my time, the Farmer's Market on West Street, between Geneva and Marquette Streets, was contained within the gutted, abandoned walls of a burnt out foundry. But as I knew it, it was simply a large empty lot where truck farmers brought their goods: rabbits, chickens, ducks, and fruits, vegetables and eggs.

I went to the Farmer's Market on Saturdays with my mother and father, and by the time I would have been old enough to go alone, it had either closed down or I had lost interest, for the reason that it was a place for shoppers, the people whose business it was to make and keep a home.

I am grateful it was there when it was, because it permitted me to see and experience many things I would have understood differently, and even experienced differently, had they happened to me when I was older. For one thing, although Wisconsin was known for its farms and dairies, its milk, cheese, corn, cows, wheat and vegetables—the making and producing of these things, as well as the nurturing that brought all of them into being—they were an unknown quantity to me.

At the Farmer's Market I saw and talked to farmers—or heard my mother and father talk to them—and so I came to know something about them, and they became a part of my expanding world, which was more than just factories and foundries, schools, sidewalks, and streets, the river and the lake, and the numerous parks, as well as the many bridges that led to these and other things.

I remember the farmers in this way: angular, mute, shy, self-conscious, and dressed always in gray. This is not meant to be an accurate portrayal, but merely the impression (of the many impressions) that became the composite picture of what I saw. That they were different from us was unmistakably. Different from the city dwellers, and certainly different from the Armenians.

The center of the lot was kept empty, with the trucks lined on each side, their tailgates down, their produce and goods stacked in boxes where they could be seen, felt, examined, tossed in the air and examined again. The animals were contained in crates, the vegetables in bushel baskets.

The place had a smell, a flavor, a taste and an odor that bordered on an aroma—that was, all in all, a perfect substance for my growing spirit.

Best of all, of course, were the living animals, and always we would take home a live chicken, my father holding it by the legs, its head hanging, facing the sidewalk, in full knowledge that its time had come.

But this did not prevent if from running madly up and down the yard, the minute it slipped from my father's grip, after its head and been severed from its neck.

On the south side of West Street, facing the

Farmer's Market, there were homes, and in the block between Geneva and Marquette Streets, in an underground, dirt floor and walled enclosure, lived Kookoolala, the town madman. He lived alone, and in silence. The only speech I ever heard him utter was a long, painful grunt, that seemed to well up from his bowels, and spoke of a suffering that was almost beyond utterance. We never bothered him when we saw him out with his wagon, gathering what he could for his solitary, mad life, but in passing his place on the way home from school, we would often taunt him—he hidden in his dark hovel, we safe on the sidewalk. And all too often he would come charging out of his den, hammer or axe in hand, and chase us, grunting and heaving, down the block.

Later, when we were in Junior High School, we encountered another of the lost, unnumbered souls, who also walked about, pulling a child's wagon, gathering, collecting, transforming the objects left scattered in the streets into something usable for his life.

This one talked, loved children, and was guileless, open, innocent, and seriously retarded.

We teased him. Or ignored him.

But he was there, as surely as we were there, his roots as deep in the earth as ours, his meaning as necessary and abiding as any of the creatures, human and not human, that God had come to manifest the earth with, for us to learn from, for Him to learn from us.

THE SLED

My bee-bee gun is the last thing I can remember owning that I didn't work for myself. This may not be true. It may have been my sled that was the last thing I didn't work for, because I can remember clearly my mother and I walking into the State Street Hardware Store and making the purchase of what had to be the finest sled anyone had ever owned—or would probably ever own—in our neighborhood. This necessity to always own the finest, the richest, the most expensive, was something that, when I think of it, was either born in me or bred into me. Or both. I am sure my mother never forgot that her family had once been rich and prominent, and perhaps she had made it her aim—whether consciously or unconsiously—to see that her son had the best she could afford.

But then, I was just as determined to move along in this direction myself.

The fancy, expensive sled was a curse. It was too big and too heavy, especially when it had to be toted up the hill. And it couldn't be thrown down easily—nor did it have the speed that the others had. The runners were also harder to work, and no amount of oil or persuasion ever got them properly loosened and free-swinging.

But it *looked* like power and performance itself. The pretense, however, was not worth the lie. For now, when I picture myself about to slam down upon my sled in preparation for the flight down the hill at the end of our block, it is always the simple racer I find myself upon, and never the other, which was the only one I ever owned.

For occasionally Jerry or Howie would switch with me, and it was their sleds that brought joy to my heart, not my own. Their sleds were small enough to be a part of the rider, and under his control, allowing him to maneuver his way swiftly and easily down the hill. And when I would rise from the borrowed sled at the bottom of the hill, I'd grab it easily with one hand and begin jostling my friends as we made our way up the hill.

Their sleds were not like this other—the one I actually owned—which had to be lugged up the hill, and required a different kind of concentration and heavy effort.

My sled helped to make me different in a way I didn't need, and it made me feel aloof, when that was not what I wanted to feel. Or, if I did, I wanted to feel it secretly, and not as a result of this appurtenance, this artifact of the ego, that made me see inescapably a part of myself I would just as soon had remained in the dark.

OUTDOORS

That's where my childhood was lived. Outdoors. I am reminded of this because of my lifelong compulsion to look out windows when I am indoors, as I have done just now, studying the black bull in the distance, beyond my hop barn window, his faultless masculine form, his quiet strength. What is there in the world of man to compare to this?

Looking out of windows caused me to remain in school two years longer than I should have. I even flunked the fifth grade twice—the second time in summer school: a torture for which my budding spirit was unprepared. I balanced the fault, if not the outrage, by quitting two years before I would have graduated from high school.

Everything took my eye to the window, and then, when spring arrived, nothing could take my eye away. The dull classroom, the dull teacher, and my fellow inmates—I was never able to understand how we had fallen into such a condition. At that time, the 1930s and 40s, there were relatively few people about, the air and the streams were clean, and the disenchantment by each of us for one another and for everything else, hadn't yet crept into the bloodstream of the human race.

I had one of two major choices once I left the indoors: Root River or Lake Michigan. Seated on my Red Racer, I remember riding to Root River but never to Lake Michigan. Was this so, or is it now just a trick of memory? I do not know. It isn't important. But it is important what I remember about riding to Root River on my bike, with my two cane poles held on my right, horizontal to the ground, and, on the left handlebar, the bucket with a can of worms inside, as well as my stringer. What I felt was shame. When I think back on it, it makes no sense, but there it was, I felt somehow demeaned by it, as if I were shabby, as if going fishing was beneath my dignity. Unfortunately, I had nothing to replace it with. If I was too good to fish for bull-heads in a muddy river, then what *was* I good for? What *did* I expect of myself?

If I rode up State Street, as I often did, I would pass Dedeh sitting in front of our church, and this would fill me with shame, not only for myself, but also for him, because he, too seemed shabby and without dignity, as he sat alone all day, involved in something as incomprehensible to me as I was sure my fishing was to everyone else.

But the drive to go fishing was strong. I wonder now if it wasn't melancholy, if the sadness I carried wasn't lodged deep in my spirit, unknown to me at the time, that I experienced only as shame.

Something drove me along. And drove me to be alone. It was something in my nature. And exploring my nature, little by little, I was beginning to find out what this something was.

WILLIAM MILLER

B
ill Miller fixed radios, traveling from home to home from his apartment on the corner of La Salle and Hamilton Streets. I can see him still, walking by himself, groomed in a well-worn suit and tie, and with an inner, imperturbable calm.

For some reason he did little repairing in his own home. We would phone him (or somehow get a message to him in the days before we had a phone) and he would come in the evening and fix our radio. Why he came in the evenings I do not know, unless of course he had another, regular full-time job, like all the other men I knew. In one or another of the factories, that is. Nor did I know that he was "colored," as we called the blacks then. I only knew that he seemed different from the other men, and for this reason I was attracted to him.

I was not any more or less attracted to him once I learned that he was colored (mulatto actually, another term from that time), because this was merely a fact to be attached *onto* him, whereas what compelled me to notice him and to go on noticing him, with that first edge of wonder and admiration that comes when we encounter a mystery, was something else: his quality of quiet dignity and pride, that I was unable not to notice.

My wonderment, if I can put it that way, was of course my own groping nature itself, for wherever I looked my eye always stopped and became attached to the non-commonplace, the thing that misfit the design. I did not put any great importance on the fact that I too was different, even though I knew I could never fit in myself. My subject of study, in the beginning at least, was not myself but others. I didn't realize then that I was looking for confirmation for myself, as well as models from whom I could learn. I was simply watching and learning—indirectly and unconsciously. The impressions I was taking were leaving a deposit that was beyond the concerns or comprehensions of my mind.

Mr. Miller—for that was his name—smoked cigars. He smoked them in a way that I had never seen before. And all cigar smoking that I have witnessed since—and for some years I was a cigar smoker myself—has been a poor approximation of the way he smoked. In that time and place, each man was known for something, and this "thing" often carried such importance that it became, for others at least, the man himself. It was therefore not surprising that he seemed legendary to me for the reason alone that he smoked his cigars with a particular expertise.

But there was more to the matter of his personalty and his influence on me than that, because in addition to smoking a cigar professionally, Mr. Miller fixed radios.

And he was colored.

And he was a bachelor and lived alone.

All of these things, in my child's mind, made him different and special.

One day I asked him about his cigar smoking. I wanted to know why I never once saw him re-light one of his cigars. He told me, in the soft-spoken way he had, that he was able to keep his cigar lit for over an hour at a time by knowing just when to puff on it, and just how *hard* to puff on it, depending on the moisture of the tobacco, the climate and temperature, and of course depending on how far down the cigar had been smoked. I was amazed and couldn't take my eyes off him. Or his cigar. I don't know what enthralled me more, the feat, or the style with which it was accomplished.

But in the end the thing that seems to lie at the basis of my remembrance of Mr. Miller is his dignity and pride. I had all along assumed that these qualities were inherent in him, but it may have been that he acquired them through suffering, and out of a deep, personal need to make something in himself that could deter prejudice and discrimination. I do not know. If this was the case then it may have been—again unconsciously—why he served as a model for me, and why in fact I admired him as much as I did.

ISLAND PARK

Openly hidden in the middle of our town, where the river stopped, turned around on itself, inhaling once, twice in a loop, before exhaling again in the direction of the factories, tanneries, and bridges of commerce, Island Park was the held breath of grace, the one complete gift of love to the city and its people.

Here everything conjoined, and at the same time was set free to go its way. It held in its arms, bridges, ball parks, pavilion, playgrounds, foot paths, lawn and picnic areas, and, of course, the boundary river itself, that gave it its name—all of it contained, uncrowded, and without the least pretension, in less than nineteen acres of space.

It was there I discovered art, and, fortunately, thought of it neither as discovery nor art, but only as wonder—for I saw in man's art his uncontrollable urge to speak intimately with nature, by holding up what he had made to mirror back what he had seen.

For there, at the bottom of Liberty Street, where it entered the park, in the backyard of the house facing the water and the bridge, was a rock garden with a bridge that was a replica in miniature of the bridge I had started to cross, and was looking back from now. My first experience of another world, the palpable world of the imagination.

There too, where I first discovered art, I learned about love, and because love came first, everything else followed. It was my earliest memory of life—my father carrying me in his arms along the worn path, with the bushes around and above me, stirring under a warm breeze. And another was there, perhaps my uncle, and something moved amongst us, a warmth of feeling, a feeling of grace, a blessing that I knew to be love.

Under that same bridge, I crabbed for bait for myself, and also to sell to the fishermen on Lake Michigan. The crabbing was best there because of the rocky bottom, where the crabs hid and waited, allowing us to coax them out with pieces of liver tied to butcher string that dangled from a cut branch, all but the latter purchased from the Boranian Grocery Store on State Street. Mr. Boranian would always wrap extra string around the white butcher paper, for he knew where we were headed. We would stand there, silently enraptured by the odors of Armenia, that oozed forth from the spices on the shelves, as well as from the opened lentil and bulghour sacks.

And once, just down river from there, I caught a small blue crappie unknown to me, that was too beautiful to be strung on a stringer, and so I rushed over the bridge and down to an abandoned dump just across from where I was fishing, and found a battered kettle that I hurried back with and placed in a depression I scraped out within the cool roots of the lilac tree just above where I was fishing. And soon I caught more of them—an entire family, that I imagined had journeyed there by accident or design, and I kept them alive in my kettle, and took them home to be seen by my mother and father, but I could not eat them and returned with them and set them free. My little brides.

Another time, with Bob and Mel Lamar, who lived at 943 Superior Street, we fished the other end of the park and caught one lone catfish that we threw on the bank, and the next day, returning to fish, he was still there, breathing, his skin shrivelled, dry, and caked with mud.

CHARLES KAMAKIAN

When we thought of him we thought of his big nose. Not that he was tall, had large feet, a broad forehead, wiry hair, powerful hands, with quick staccato movements—but that he had a big nose.

Each person had a chief, identifying feature, and this was what he was known by, even though it was seldom mentioned. Although, being young, cruel, heartless and dumb, it was—it was very often mentioned.

Perhaps it was simply our astonishment, our own way of cataloging the unusual in order to make a fitting, composite and reasonable picture of life—even though, as we all knew life was not reasonable, even if we quakingly hoped it might turn out to be intelligible once we grew up.

In the meantime, there were the streets, and the forms that moved about in the streets, and of that tribe we too were numbered.

Also we had names.

This is how we responded intelligently to our astonishment.

For as long as anyone could remember, Chuck Kamakian was called Horse. I believe it was Eggs Kirkorian or Kush Kashian who gave him that name, but then who gave them their names?

It didn't matter. It was the named, not the namer, that was important.

It would be another thirty years or more before I

realized that Horse—or Chuck, or Charley, or Raz—
was handsome, and had a host of qualities and features
I was only subliminally aware of at the time. Least of
which was his nose, although his nose was also fitting,
and—after all, worthy of mention—and not at all big
for his general size, and did, if anything, benefit, not
distract, from his handsomeness, however much it
might have once undermined his pride.

GERALD HANSEN

Jerry Hansen was a Dane, and the only one with whom I felt a deep and abiding kinship. Our homes were no more than 150 yards apart, the back door of his house on La Salle Street facing diagonally the back door of our house on Superior Street. All the back yards in those days were common thoroughfares.

There was a chemical antipathy between the Danes and the Armenians. The Danes comprised nearly a third of the population of Racine, and we felt surrounded, if not engulfed by them, as they must have felt encroached upon, if not contaminated by us. We were a highly unlikely combination, and it was probably the common thread of poverty alone that made co-existence possible.

But perhaps Jerry was something also not Danish, as I was no doubt something also not Armenian. It may have been that he was not satisfied with the conditions and limitations of being a Dane; or, being poor and living next door to a large apartment house, rented exclusively to "coloreds"—among whom he also made friends—his chemistry, willy-nilly, began to blend with the chemistries of others not like himself.

Or perhaps it was something else: loneliness, compassion, or a curious, sensitive and easygoing nature.

The two-story house that Jerry shared with his extended family, consisted of his five brothers, three sisters, his parents, an aunt and an uncle (neither married), and a grandmother, with the unlikely name of Danny.

Jerry shared the attic with his uncle Muncie, who was known as Madman Munce. I never visited the attic, but years later, when we were drafted into the Army, I can remember Jerry's amazement at having sheets to sleep on for the first time in his life.

He was of medium height, stocky, crew cut blond, with a nature that was open, trusting, and fearless.

Above all, he was casual, and gave one the feeling that he had time for everything. This very openness made him take to and become interested in all manner of things. What I took to be strange, confused, mixed-up and bewildering, and therefore needed to be struggled with, was, for Jerry, just another manifestation of the unknowable and yet habitable pattern of life.

Where I was closed, Jerry was open, and he went out easily to the one commodity that was free—the experience of other people.

And he was free of the past—and perhaps it was this, more than anything, that caused me to seek his friendship, because it was this that allowed his nature, which was fundamentally good, to be open, unwary, relaxed, and ready to greet each new experience with a smile of acceptance. In short, he was all the things the circumstances of my life did not permit me to be. I had opened—and would continue to keep myself open—to nature, but something in my inheritance kept me from trusting others.

Whether fishing on the pier, swimming at the quarry or lake, or driving in a car or bus, if Jerry became tired and decided to take a nap, he would merely curl himself in ball, close his eyes and enter instantly that other world, that he seemed never to fear.

The dark clouds of brooding and suspicion that followed me, did not follow Jerry. Diving off the pier, or off the wall ledge of the quarry, it seemed his head emerged from the water at the same time his feet went under. I could picture his body taking the shape of a half-moon, and I can still see his fingertips emerging as his feet went underwater. But this was simply the way he did things: totally relaxed and completely present. I knew I couldn't imitate him, so I merely looked on in wonder.

Being disappointed with ordinary life and unsatisfied with people who were average, I had, of course, to make heroes. Above all, I felt that I was growing incorrectly because of the lack of suitable models. "Why are there no great men here," my mother remembered my asking her, when I was a mere ten years old.

"Because of the Turks," she had answered. "They killed off all our greatest men."

"How about the Americans, then? What's their excuse?"

Interestingly, I remember only the accusation, not the exact words. And the place: State Street, between Marquette Street and Milwaukee Avenue.

Were we waiting for a bus, or had I merely stopped our walk long enough to make the accusation? Perhaps it was that I remember streets in the way I can never remember talk—the cheapness of words, their pettiness. Our lies.

But the streets never lied. They told a rough, violent and busy truth to all who lived there. And it was in the streets that I was born, and where my outer life would find its enaction, as my inner life would continue to be nurtured by nature.

I went fishing. I waited. And I had a friend, who— although I did not know it then—would leave an indelible mark on my life.

THE GREEK POPCORN MAN

The name of the Greek popcorn man was Philip. This I learned many years later. But all the years I knew him I never once heard his name used. The reason for this was simple: he didn't speak, nor was he spoken to.

If I go back in memory, I can perhaps recollect his talking while making a transaction—but nothing more. As a rule, we simply slid our money forward on the short counter, the money advanced indicating the size of bag we wanted.

I don't think I thought of him as having a name. Certainly not the name Philip.

He meant two things to me specifically. One, he was part of the American landscape, part of those teenage evenings of ball parks, arc lights, and awakening sex. And then, being Greek, being foreign born and swarthy, I identified him with my own people. I was embarrassed for him and embarrassed because of him, for I felt deep inside that he was being compromised.

In life all things find their level and their function—with intention, if the man is wise, but unintentionally, if he is not, for nature will always be served. But either way, a balance is made and we look out (as children) at the workings of man and nature, and we perceive the world as being in harmony. More or less.

But occasionally the pattern is violently disrupted, and a man who does not seem to be where he should be, is, nevertheless, there, and our sensibility is disturbed, and (as children) we are not quite sure what went wrong.

Did I think he belonged in the factories with the other immigrant workers? Or was I simply disturbed because someone, so much like the elders of my own community, was invading territory where the ritual drama of my puberty was being enacted? Was I embarrassed? And if so, was I embarrassed for him, or because I knew that the configurations of the drama I was involved in were American, not Armenian, that the soil I was inhabiting and repossessing nightly with my own coming manhood, was America's, not Armenia's, and that—like it or not—one would have to be repudiated for the other.

I was making a choice, I thought and it seemed to me at the time that I had turned my back on the old world and was slowly, imperceptibly entering the world of the new.

Or was it just my own youth? And did he represent merely old age? something in all this was not very clear.

It had something to do with this being America, not Armenia, and it had something to do with the guilt of that and the guilt I was made to feel about sex. I didn't know then what neurosis was—in people or in nations. I had a lot to learn, but slowly, slowly, I was beginning to find out.

LOTCH OGLANIAN

His real name was Khatchik Koroghlanian, but he was never known by that name outside his immediate family. He was called Harry in school, but only by the teachers. This was the name he had given them upon their insistence that he have an "American" name, like everyone else. Where he got the name Harry I cannot imagine, because it did not suit him, and every time I heard it used something inside me cringed.

It was around this time, when we were in the third or fourth grade, that Bud Graham gave him his true name—Lotch. How Bud came up with that name I do not know. Up until that moment Lotch had been swimming in the solution of his personality, that was still very much in formation, but at that magic moment something crystallized and his identity became fixed. A name can do that.

From then on he became a permanent fixture in our neighborhood and a member of our gang, whose principal figures were Jerry Hansen, Howie Sell, Bud Graham, Lotch, Naz Gengozian, and myself.

For some reason Lotch had a reputation for being stupid.

He had been cast for the role and he had no choice but to play it. He played it quietly and humbly, because that was his nature, and he played it stoically, as well, for the same reason.

His center of gravity was in his body, not his

head, and his physique was nearly model perfect. He was also the best all-around athlete in the school, the strongest boy, the quietest, as I have already said—and, having become even quieter because of the tag of stupidity, he became in time almost inscrutable, as he drew further and further inside himself.

It embarrassed him to be called stupid, and I believe in the end he came to believe it.

He was also admired and feared, and, as I have already implied, he was honored because of his physical prowess, because of his inherent ability to blend strength with grace.

But behind his back we called him Einstein, and to his face *Ein*stein. The cruelty of children, the stupidity of children.

GIDEON COURT

Every street had a personality, a character of its own. And although it would be inaccurate to say that each street had its own style, it was nevertheless true that there was something in the streets that taught one style, for each street was unique, and had to be responded to in a different way.

To walk down broad and ample Milwaukee Avenue was not the same as walking briskly up La Salle Street, or sauntering quietly along Prospect.

Each street offered something different, and each was the owner of a different class and style of people. But for those who were in the streets it was the same; for the ones who walked them were not always the ones who lived in them.

We walked West Street to Garfield School, La Salle Street to Washington Junior High, and we rode or drove to Horlick High School using these streets, as well as others.

The neighborhood streets we often marked for fruit trees and vegetable gardens, that we would raid in the summer months.

Best of all, of course, were the streets where we played, and where, moving along alone, one discovered, little by little, the different homes, the nature of people, the character of their lives—and, most interesting of all, the odd and strange structures that were somehow so personal and individual that they instantly belonged to everyone. I am thinking of the odd-shaped garages, the old store fronts, the uninhabited buildings that once housed businesses, fire stations, or served as warehouses, but that now seemed to be without a noticeable function. Much of the city's history had not yet been effaced, but was dying slowly of inertia and want of proper use.

Did one wonder who the architects of streets were? Was a city designed, or did it grow according to the needs of the people? Why was Superior Street, for example, chopped into four separate blocks, running north in a jagged line, until it petered out at the edge of town.

I finally decided that it couldn't have been done by blueprint—that a city was not created the way a building or a park was—or a bridge—but that it just happened, the same way that the people happened upon it, and to it. I believe I came to this conclusion because of Gideon Court, which was no more than a block away from my house.

It was a narrow, red brick-lined passageway, just wide enough for a single car, and had a T-square shape, the horizontal bar extending into La Salle Street at one end, and West Street at the other, and with the vertical bar emptying in a decline onto Prospect Street.

There were homes crowded everywhere into its half block by quarter block lengths, and somehow, because of the cramped space, one had to consider each dwelling separately.

Everyone who lived there seemed a little strange, including an Armenian family, that never fitted—or wanted to fit—with either the Armenians or the Americans.

Bud Graham lived there with his large, Irish family.

Only one house had a formal garden, while all the others seemed cramped for space. All of the people that ever lived there seemed reclusive and withdrawn, but I don't believe the place made them that way, I believe it was because of their temperament that they came to live there in the first place.

And what of the temperament of the person or people who created this uninhabitable, and yet, somehow, mysteriously, habitable place? Was it an odd family, "just off the boat," as we used to say, or was it originally used for some other purpose? Apparently the razed building on the corner, at La Salle Street, was a clue, because it remained in rubble all the years I lived there, until finally it wore itself into an open pathway.

Nevertheless, I wasn't all that curious about any of it at the time, especially since I walked it everyday to school, and used it for a shortcut at other times, on my way to Root River, or to visit Chuck Kamakian. In time, it became for me one of the curious facts of the city, as I slowly, slowly, adjusted—or almost adjusted—to the oddities and curiosities of life, never feeling quite at home, never knowing quite what home was, or how it could be found.

JOE PERCH

I learned a great deal about art and style from Joe Perch. Also patience, silence, humility, and method. But the thing he really represented for me was the one thing he could not teach: class.

I think I need to clarify what I mean by teaching and learning.

Perhaps it would be better to say that I witnessed these things in Joe Perch and that this witnessing became the influence under which I unknowingly learned.

It is significant that he did not do anything the way anyone else did.

In time he had his imitators, but none of them being artists, they adopted only his methods. These they applied in their own desultory fashion, limited by their understanding—which was, at best, partial.

The standard method of fishing for (not necessarily *catching*) perch, was this: fish out at the end of the pier, use catgut only for the leader, weight your line, hook your minnow (or crab tail) through the back (which instantly killed the minnow), and either jig your pole or fish it under or attached to your seat, so it wouldn't move. Never use a cork.

Except for the oddball fishermen who used trolley lines, everyone fished with cane poles.

This was both the one thing we had in common with Joe Perch, as well as our point of departure.

Joe Perch fished close in towards shore, where the

pier had been shored up by boulders. He used catgut only for his lines, and tiny bottle corks, with household matches inserted to hold the line to the cork, and he hooked his minnows under their spines, so they would stay alive. Hook and minnow were the only weight on Joe's lines, and because the water was usually choppy close in towards shore, his minnows often rode up high, just under the roiling waves—thereby causing them to behave very much as living minnows would.

There was something thrilling about watching his corks disappear under the waves the minute he had one on. So different from river fishing, where the cork would jump up and down, and only later be pulled under (if it was a bullhead or catfish), or run along in jabs and starts, before going under (if it was a rock bass or crappie). But perch were decisive, which was maybe their attraction for Joe Perch, who was just as decisive, not to mention single-minded and faultless in his pursuit.

He always had a stringer of fish. Always! And he never spoke, never bragged, never complained—and never explained.

He just caught fish.

He was everybody's hero on the pier, adult and child alike. He stood for something, but I don't think we ever understood what that something was.

Say it was class, say it was style, as I say now that he was the first artist I ever saw at work. And this perhaps explains his silence, because he had to do his work out in the open, where it could be watched and seen by others.

But somehow his inner world was never affected by this. He went about his business, which as anyone could see, was catching fish . . . and yet, there was something else involved, something much deeper, something much, much deeper than catching perch in a lake on a line.

UMBAJI PARK

I am sure there was a lore that went with every one of the tiny parks that dotted our city, but the park and its lore that was also somehow a part of my own lore was Umbaji Park.

Umbaji, whose name meant foreman in Turkish, was an Armenian.

Colbert was the official name of the park, but it had never been called that, as far as I know, although I can remember a time when it was called Bum's Park. That must have been before Umbaji took up full-time residence.

It was located at the end of Prospect Street, which was the street at the bottom of our dead end block. From the bottom of Superior Street—below where it dead ended—Prospect Street ran for another half block to Douglas Avenue, and then another short block—the entire north side of the street being occupied by St. Patrick's Church—where it ended at Umbaji Park.

Sitting on a knoll, in the shadow of St. Patrick's Church, Umbaji Park overlooked the State Street and Main Street bridges, and—in the distance—Lake Michigan. It was a tiny park that sloped at a 45 degree angle, and it was shaped in a triangle. The one bench—that Umbaji freely moved about—was often at the top of the park, from where it commanded a full view of all that I have described.

At the bottom of the hill there was a drinking

fountain bordering the sidewalk, and a low tubular fence and shrub bushes, as protection, because the park at this point was built above the street, there being no sidewalk at the base of the "triangle."

Because of the way it was situated, it provided a commanding view of the city, the river, and of the populace—as it passed by foot and car and boat.

But I don't think Umbaji chose his park for any of these reasons.

He had come to Racine in 1910 to make money to return to the homeland with, as so many Armenians before him had done. He was unable to return because of the war, and when his wife was killed in the Turkish Massacres, he was too old to start another life in America. With no home or promise or future, he came in time to make this tiny, insignificant park his final resting place

His name, I found out much later, was Hovhannes Pahltahlian, and, like my father, he was from Adana, although his ancestors had come from Tomarza, as my father's had come from Kharpet.

Although I saw him several times a week during the summer months, I don't believe I ever heard him speak.

It was said he washed his clothes in the fountain, slept on the bench, and relieved himself in the bushes. This was the lore of the park—a legend created by children and later perpetuated by adults.

But I had been there as a witness to the man, not the legend.

Walking to Lake Michigan in the early morning, cane poles in one hand, a bucket of crabs in the other, I always stopped for a drink at the fountain, the water fresh, clean and cold, as it bubbled ceaselessly over the perforated brass ball, and tumbled over tiny pebbles of white and brown. While I drank I stared at the pebbles and inhaled the aroma of the fountain, its damp, cool smell seeming to be the earthy soul of the wet fountain itself.

Umbaji was always in sight, sitting or lying on his bench, mute, listless, and gray. I knew he was Armenian, I knew he had no work, and I knew very little else.

I would straighten from the fountain, bang my poles on the sidewalk to align their bottoms, turn and go on my way.

DEDEH

Dedeh, I was to find out much later, meant Grandfather in Turkish. It could also mean Father of the race, in which case the name could be taken as a title, or as an earned honor—and acquired name that effaced the given name of the man.

I was not aware of it at the time, but Dedeh, I am sure, had been named in this way.

He was in no way noble or outstanding. Nor was he distinguished, or in any way special. And yet, as the accumulation of lived moments coalesce and pass gradually into memory, what emerges from my own remembrance is a man who possessed all of these qualities, along with the still greater quality of humility.

He was, I believe now, all of these things because he was none of them. He was none of them because he thought of himself as nothing. I don't think he even thought of himself as simple or unimportant. Perhaps he thought of himself as insignificant.

It was because of this right attitude—that is possessed by so few, and understood and valued by even fewer—that he was able to find his function, which he had assumed, I am sure, without appointment, and had fulfilled without any special thanks.

I don't remember if I ever spoke to him, but whenever I rode my bike up State Street, he would be there, sitting on his metal folding chair, mornings and afternoons, in front of the doors of St. Mesrob Armenian Church.

Traveling west from home, I would pass first the fire station, and wave to the blue uniformed firemen, sitting in threes and fours on their sturdy wooden chairs. They would wave back and call out, and I would be proud to be recognized by men whose badges flashed so brilliantly in the sun.

And then, just next door, I would see Dedeh again, in his old clothes, seated, serene and silent, and I would look away and bicycle on.

Sundays he would stand in front of the church and enter with the last of the parishioners. But all week he kept his vigil alone, nodding to his countrymen as they passed, as he did to those who occasionally entered the doors he sat beside.

The meek shall inherit the earth, the Bible says. Dedeh had inherited his portion of it while he lived.

He grows more understandable and cherishable with each passing year.

OUR GANG

It is worth remembering the calls that came from outside the home—the outside callers that called the insiders out.

We were sensitive to the sounds of the night, our companion's voices, and we would always respond at once.

Often to the dismay of our parents, because any outside voice pitched high enough to be heard was a call to the Great Outdoors.

It meant play, activity, an occurrence between friends, its urgency demanding that all available bodies collect beneath the familiar street lights, where our bodies, the night, and the unending energies of life coalesced and gave form to the ritual dance of childhood.

This was our immortality, and never for us was it ordinary or predictable, for we never lived in anticipation of the hour, but rather, we lived in the moment itself, never looking forward, never looking back.

We were the Gods of the Night, the chosen ones, the ones that balanced all opposites by keeping everything stirred and active and in solution—for out of this something new would always emerge.

There were voices anonymous, unhurried, and voices urgent and demanding, for each block and neighborhood had its gang, and its own way of calling.

And so I remember again the intentional calling out—by Bud and Jerry and me, by Howie and Chuck and Lotch.

Scenario: All of us but one have gathered under the street light.

"Let's get Howie," one of us hollers, and off we go.

"Oooohh Hoowieeeee," we'd shout at the mute house, where inside the law of adult life transpired in open, unfathomable secrecy.

"Oooohh Hoowiieee," we would croon again, stretching the words that they ease through wood and plaster walls, inspiring our comrade to free himself from the evil clutches of family love.

And then suddenly Howie would bolt out the door and we would be off, racing for adventure.

Or, on another occasion, he would open the door and stand between us and the light, placing his hat on his head, and then taking it off—before finally speaking. "My mom said to tell you I can't come out. I'm behind in my chores and Lois is sick again."

"So what's that got to do with you?" and than in a lowered voice, "Can't you sneak out?"

"How am I gonna sneak out? Jeez! My dad would strap me. Honest guys, I can't come out."

Bud: "We're gonna raid old man Kherdian's garden. Dave says it's okay. Tell 'em Dave."

Dave: "It's okay."

Jerry: "You're the only one missing. Can't you say you're coming to my house to study our encyclopedia?"

No answer. Universal disbelief.

Howie: "Lay off, you guys. I can't come, that's all."

Howie's mother: "Are those hoodlums still out there? You just close that door now and come inside."

We all shuffle and fuss, all of us, that is, but Jerry, who knows what is possible, what is not. "Can I sleep with you on the roof tonight?"

"Sure," Howie whispers through the cracked door.

"Too bad," Lotch says. "Too bad you can't make it, Howie. We'll be thinking of you Ots."

"The nights still young, Ots," I pitch in, "you can always sneak out later."

JUNIOR ROGNERUD

Of the neighborhood boys, the boys of the block, the playmates I grew up with that were my friends for a time, the one I needed most as a balance for my own heavy nature was Junior Rognerud. He was sloppy, carefree, open and unafraid. He wasn't going anywhere, never felt out of place, and seemed neither confused nor disturbed—by his life or anyone else's.

Because he didn't judge things, everything passed through him, uncolored, untainted, whole.

One day he said to me, "Our mothers hatched us like eggs."

"Like a chicken?" I countered, flabbergasted.

"They hatched us just like chickens hatch their eggs," he explained, without any noticeable feeling.

At that time, age seven or eight, I had been giving a lot of thought to where I had come from, but never about how I had gotten here.

I ran home and told my mother, who was, if anything, more flabbergasted than I was. But differently. She wondered if the influence of the home would ever be able to stand up to the corruption of the streets.

OUR BLOCK

There were a number of streets that had as many Armenian families living on them as ours, but only in our neighborhood—or, to be more exact, our section of the city.

The Armenian children, many of whom were playmates of mine, were the easiest for me to understand. For one thing, we spoke the language of Armenia in our homes—with different accents, and varying mixtures of Turkish blended in (or spoken exclusively by our parents, when they didn't want us to understand), and we sometimes spoke in the mother tongue to each other, when we wanted to keep something from our non-Armenian (*odar*) playmates.

Also, we ate the same foods at home, slept under the same covers—called *yourghans* (woolen quilts), shared the same values of frugality, suspicion, common sense, truth telling (within reason), respect for our elders, honesty (up to a point), shrewdness, and, above all, we valued money, education, family solidarity, and love of God.

Despite all this, we fought with each other anyhow. But not seriously, because, being members of a common tribe, it was difficult to hold a grudge, or even to stay mad with one's friend when you liked his mother, or respected his older brother, or had once received a favor from some other member of his family.

We also believed in gratitude and manners.

It was different with the *odars*, who we usually

referred to as the "Americans." Anyone whose parents were born in this country, if they weren't as dark (or darker) than us, we called Americans. We were of course the Armenians, although when the Americans were angry with us, or wished to insult us, they called us Harmones, or Dirty Armenians. The latter expression both pained and confused me. Why *dirty*, when our living habits—based on my observations, at least— were far cleaner than were those of the Americans, who were often defeated by poverty, and were—very often—the last to own radios, telephones, refrigerators, and other "modern" appliances. Our next door neighbor not only used our telephone, they sent their child over to our house once a week for a tub bath, as well.

So why were they insulting us in this way? I finally concluded that it was because we were dark, and dark in their minds meant dirty.

I didn't want to be blond. On the other hand I didn't want to be any darker than Tyrone Power. He was—in a way—dark like us, although lighter complected, and with features not at all Mediterranean. But he did have black, black hair.

One of our neighbors, Zary Kaiserlian, announced one day that Tyrone Power was an Armenian. *Blood and Sand*, in technicolor, starring Tyrone Power and Rita Hayworth, had been showing at the Venetian Theater for the second straight week. Rouben Mamoulian, who *was* Armenian, was the director. "Why he give such big role him, if he not Armenian, ha! Explain me that." Her *odar* neighbors took no notice of her, while all her Armenian friends were eager to be convinced.

But it was no use. We couldn't make ourselves more desirable by making Tyrone Power Armenian. We were stuck with ourselves the way we were. We could maybe change the color of our hair, but never the color of our skin.

I had no choice in the end but to begin to live with these feelings of inferiority that were being imposed on me, and there were times when I was tempted to believe the slander, but two things kept this from happening: One, the Americans were notably not special in any way (their only claim to superiority was their majority), and two, our parents were so haughty and superior in their belief in the Armenian character—in its integrity, resilience and fortitude, that they were somehow able to instill in us a pride in our heritage.

But stretched in this way, between two quite distant poles, our sensibilities were strained, and we became awkward and apologetic and self-effacing, despite ourselves, and the membrane of sensitivity, having developed too soon, was forced either into a posture of bragging, lying, or withdrawal, which often manifested in wounded pride.

Some of us pushed too hard, fell on our faces, got up and pushed again, while others withdrew into the safety and shelter of their homes, and were never able to re-emerge and engage again in the great American experiment and dream.

None of us were normal.

And yet our parents would admonish us in their inimitable English, "Don't be abnormal, you (pronounced *ahpnormel*). "You going grow up be zero."

Had we only been Armenian we might not have become *ahpnormel*. But had we been only Armenian we wouldn't have been forced to be more than we were. We were being pushed into a larger world, and it was the other children of our block who were our entry into that world, like it or not.

There was a great deal to be gained or lost.

I gave up all hope of feeling entirely good or entirely bad about myself, and threw myself into the life around me with abandon. And yet, the best part of my life, the secret part, the part I kept for myself alone, I opened only to nature. For my love of nature was something beyond like and dislike, as well as beyond my immediate comprehension. Nature was the source of all mystery and wonder. I never tired of it, and it seemed never to grow tired of me.

HERBERT VON HADEN

No doubt Mr. Von Haden is still alive. Although he seemed to me, at age eleven or twelve, to be as old as any adult could or *should* be, I realize now that he was probably a young man, perhaps in his thirties, when he became the principal of Garfield School.

Along with his appointment as principal, he assumed the role of coach for our softball and basketball teams. Our janitor, Gustave Sheibach, whom we called Shypoke, was the unofficial coach of our softball team, working with us every recess, and coaching from the sidelines at all our games. I don't think he ever attended a basketball game, however.

But none of this is the important thing, and it may even be that there is nothing of importance or interest in any of this, but I don't believe this is true. I believe the opposite is true, but the reason I am floundering and do not know quite how to begin this sketch is because Mr. Von Haden's qualities, as well as the quality he brought to our lives, is difficult to define.

So let me try again, but not by beginning there, but by saying that our grab bag lives were cluttered by great mixtures of types and ethnic groups, with all their various predispositions, but that the common, undeniable ingredient was poverty—poverty of means, but not of spirit.

But the spirit cannot soar if it is bound by serious physical or material limitations. Instead of soaring, the spirit remains cramped and coarse. We, the Armenians, suffered the further limitation of being the offspring of peasant immigrants, whereas the "Americans" were simply and undeniably coarse, for reasons I was unprepared to understand at the time.

Under these confused and conflicting circumstances, the teachers took to hating, despising, or, at best, condescending to the Armenian children. We didn't speak English the way the other children did—it being, after all, or second language, for Armenian was the only language spoken in most of our homes. And we had strange, unpronounceable names, that we were all to eager to forfeit, if it would do any good—all the while hating our parents for having made such a blunder in the first place. Because my name was David, I received the obverse of this prejudice—the other Armenian children began calling me by the Armenian version of my name—*Tavit*—and this name was soon taken up by the others, so that I too was made to suffer from a similar embarrassment.

The fact that we were proud and arrogant made it even worse. Who did we think we were to be disdainful of those who condescended to correct us, and who were working as mercifully as possible to deliver us into the gracious world of Anglo-Saxon America.

Into this strange malaise and mixture strode Herbert Von Haden, all six feet, six inches of him, in his dark, pinstriped suits, bow ties, and black, pointed shoes.

Not once, not ever, did he look down on us because we were a little backward in our manners, smelled of garlic, wore hand-me-down clothes, were shy and fearful (of authority, in particular), spoke English with a strange idiomatic twist, and often got to the top by pushing a little harder than everyone else.

I think he liked us because we *were* achievers, because we had in abundance what he too had in abundance—vitality and an uncontrollable emotional center.

In his own way he exploded as often as we did, and although our respect for him bordered on awe (because he respected us in turn), it wasn't this that made us accept his outbursts without question, but rather that his outbursts were no different than our own, except that he had the authority and ability to push what he believed and desired into completion.

Once, for example, he literally kicked Lotch Oglanian off the bench and into the basketball game at Douglas Park, because we were behind in a game we could not afford to lose. That kick alone may have been the reason we won that game. He was more frightening than the opposition, but since we had nothing *really* to fear in him we had nothing to fear in either the opposition *or* ourselves.

He made us believe we were okay. And all at once he neutralized the warring forces that were, of course, nothing more than the anxieties everyone felt—from

teachers to pupils to parents to leaders, or semi-lead-
ers—because none of us were quite at home where we
were, and it was natural to feel that something or
someone was at fault. But the force of his presence had
made a kind of grace, and brought an understanding
that he alone was responsible for.

And then, just as suddenly as he had arrived, he
was gone.

A benevolent tornado had come and gone, leaving in its wake a great hole that we would have to fill
by ourselves. But he had left us with the means and the
confidence that we could.

THE RUNAWAY

I began running away from home sometime after the age of ten.

I would walk up State Street after dusk, and stop, as a rule, at the pool hall and cigar store around the corner on Main Street. I might watch the pool players for awhile—or, if the owner threw me out, browse among the comics or paperback novels, whose covers contained barefooted Southern women, whose pretty faces were held up to the reader in a provocative pout or leer.

And then I would go home.

After a few years I began to notice the pattern. Even before I left the house I knew I would be returning home—well before morning.

But I couldn't give up *wanting* to run away, nor could I overcome the particular feeling of hurt that caused this compulsion in me to flee from home.

It only happened when I was hurt in a particular way. It occurred when I felt that something private in me had been outraged. It had to do with my true self not being understood, which caused me to feel violated.

My poor soul sensed its true state of homelessness and wanted to flee.

And then one day I realized that this life that seemed to have been thrust upon me could not be exchanged for another, truer life. What I needed had to be made. By me. And the time for that making had not arrived.

MADZOON

Etched deep into the groove of memory is my mother's yogurt sack, dripping incessantly under the kitchen sink.

Today we have cupboards under our sinks, to hide the elbow as it wends its way downstairs into the mysterious entrails of plumbing—but then, in childhood's home, it was there, as naked as our need, as urgent as our lives.

The sink, the bare elbow, and the dripping, fermenting yogurt (called *madzoon* by us, years before yogurt, a Turkish word, was coined by the Americans).

Then we would scoop it out of the cheesecloth sack mother had placed it in, and into a porcelain bowl, and from there we would spread it over our *dolmas* and *sarmas* and *kuftas*, and then, at the end of the meal (or after school), we'd dish it into a saucer, sprinkle sugar over it, and eat it for dessert.

If money is the common denominator of the rich, food is the common denominator of the poor.

Thus we ate and thus it was made and thus it looked as it drained, daily, hourly—instilling its ingredients into our lives, as it dripped endlessly into the waiting pan below the elbow of the sink.

It was wonderful. It was there. It was us and we were it, and if you are what you eat, then I am maybe one-third *madzoon*, and the other two-thirds doesn't matter.

MR. ROGNERUD

J unior Rognerud's father owned a filling station on the corner of State and Marquette Streets, next to the Armenian coffee house beside Garfield School.

Will the reader believe me if I say that owning a filling station at that time was out of the ordinary? Well it was!

At least I thought so, and I'm sure all my friends thought so, too.

Mr. Rognerud was a businessman, a man with a calling, and with work that he himself had arranged.

The other thing that was impressive about him was that he seldom spoke. This proved that he was somebody, because he was not silent out of melancholy, as so many of my own people were, but out of a natural pride and dignity that came with being self-employed and self-assured.

These were the kinds of thoughts that I had going on in my head at the time.

Whenever I walked by his station I would look up and see his name engraved on the sign above the door. It wasn't just another name, it was the name of the man I knew who lived on my block, whose son was my friend, etc.

I liked all the Rogneruds—looked up to them: their blondness, their sturdiness, their assurance in a world that they or their forebearers had made.

Did I wonder what my destiny would be? Did I wonder if I *had* a destiny?

Yes and no.

Mostly I was just taking everything in. Watching and waiting.

I was content for the moment just to be alive.

SWINGS

Then there were the girls on swings—gently gliding back and forth.

It was Geneva Street that summer, and it was the summer boyhood ended.

Little wonder that it was held in that single image of girls in summer shorts, gently gliding—up, down and back—while we stood on the sidewalk, entranced.

Something had ended, something had—almost—begun. Forever after it would be entwined with unnamed and forgotten friends, and street lights (their towering strength), shielding but lighting the girls who had suddenly ceased to giggle, while the fireflies blinked in the distance, the crickets chirped, and the whispering night held us swaying in its secret arms.

CARPENTERS

There were always older people living in the house next to ours. One, an old German couple, I remember only vaguely, but I have used that memory as a metaphor in several of my poems.

Perhaps I should not call it memory, but association.

The old man liked to build, and often, when I would awaken in the morning, he would be out in back, sawing. My bedroom was at the back of the house and faced the back of theirs. I think it was the summer air, the warmth of the sun, the feeling of freedom and adventure, the sense of not knowing what the day would bring, only that it was glorious to be alive, on one's feet, and rushing into one's clothes, for nearly always I would throw open my window and inhale the morning air and the perfume of my mother's purple and yellow irises, growing under my window, and perhaps I would either see or hear the old man at his work, and sense in him and his activity an affinity with my own.

I think it was something like that.

And it was probably why I thought, later, that I wanted to be a carpenter. Perhaps it would awaken me to myself, as it had once awakened me to life.

THE FISHERMEN

I do not remember a time when we used the dilapidated garage at the back of our yard. For as long as I can remember, Bill Zaehler, our next door neighbor, rented it from my parents for 50 cents a month. Inside, he kept his minnow and crab tanks, and his large fishing nets, that were lined in the back—after being poled out to dry in his long, narrow yard. His back yard was identical in size to ours, but, unlike ours—which was full of trees and vegetables, flowers and a grape arbor—his consisted of struggling patches of grass, flourishing weeds, and a well-worn path between his home and our garage, which faced his yard.

Here, he and his fishing relatives talked, cleaned fish, and dried their nets. The yard belonged, as well, to Bill's dog, Bozo, a mean fox-terrier, who barked at everyone who entered his domain, and never tired of biting my ankles.

He knew of course who belonged to the yard and who did not.

But there was another, easier way to get rid of me.

"Perch are running, Dave," Bill would would say, as I stood, open-mouthed, watching the men pulling perch and trout from their nets.

They *are*, Uncle Bill," I would answer, incredulous, never suspecting.

"Joe Perch went home an hour ago with a stringer full."

"But he always catches a stringer full, Uncle Bill."

"They're running, Dave! I tell you, they're running. Boys at the weather station say there's a storm blowing in. Winds'll be shifting south any minute. You know what that means."

"Blow the bait into the fish's mouth," I'd answer, and without another word, I'd dash into my back yard and grab my two cane poles, that I kept tied under the rain pipe where our roof line declined and stopped just above my head.

Did the fish ever once run when Bill said they would? Had he even once been to the pier and watched the fishermen, before coming home and making his pronouncement? And did I ever notice a change in the weather once I got to the pier?

I doubt it, because looking back, I think it was a mutually supportive game. No one could not enjoy teasing a child that was as incredulous as I, and since we both loved fishing, I'm sure he enjoyed seeing me go off—and seeing me return, even if I had nothing more to show for my effort than three or four perch.

I can see him now, laughing to himself. His big grin and dancing eyes. He was a good tease—the right kind of tease, because he never laughed *at* anyone. The joke was life itself, its vagaries and mysteries—and he had let himself in for the ride.

And his grin said: Anyone can be in on it, just join up before life passes by.

My father, too, was a fisherman of sorts.

Perhaps it was he who taught me to fish, but I doubt it.

I was born to fish, and I cannot remember a time when I did not fish. In fact, I date my memory by this fact, because all of my remembrances before I was a fisherman are fuzzy, except for one in particular, which is etched on my soul.

I must have been four years old. We were on our way to the picnic grounds at the end of Lincoln Field. My uncle was driving his Model-A Ford, my father beside him, while my mother and I sat quietly in back.

As we entered the park and drove alongside the river, I spotted two fishermen standing in the river, where the water moved back and forth across their knees. They were waving what looked like magic wands, that I knew somehow were magical poles. The river sparkled, reflecting the warm rays of he the sun, and rippled as it rushed below the men. It seemed to be blue, white and golden all at once. And I knew in an instant what all of it meant, that there were living beings in the water that these men were trying to catch. But more than the fish, and more than the fishermen, I was spellbound by the water—the ultimate mystery, the life before life, that I was certain now had brought me here.

I was seeing Root River for the very first time.

No substance or meaning would ever enter deeper into the heart of my being. I would follow its course all of my young life, from the State Street bridge, where I next encountered it, to the dam, far outside town—and then, above the dam and beyond; and as I traveled to other rivers and cities, all the rivers became extensions of this river, and all the cities extensions of this city, for the meaning of life had begun for me in the form and ritual of these two fishermen, their lines dripping beads of water, as they whipped their rods up from the water's surface and then laid their lines back down.

LAKE MICHIGAN

Although Racine (which meant Root in French) came to its location because of the river, it was, nevertheless, the river in conjunction with the lake that made it a valuable and viable setting.

But first the river had to be dredged and cleaned of its roots.

Later, piers were put in to break the waves, with a foghorn at the end of the north pier, and then, further out, a lighthouse station, that was called Reef Light.

The true lighthouse was located at the furthest northern reach of the territory that we thought of as *our place*—outside of the city proper, perhaps, but part of the city of our mind.

There was a pier just south of the lighthouse, a golf course above it, and in the parking lot that served the golf course and picnic grounds, we sometimes parked at night with our teenage dates and watched the "submarine races."

Beyond the lighthouse was no-man's land, but if you took the highway north from there you would eventually reach Milwaukee, where the lake would again come into view.

The Danes, who comprised nearly one-third of our population of 70,000, lived on the West Side, and everyone else lived either north or south. There was no east side. It belonged to the lake.

If a stranger asked where east was, we would answer, "That way, till your hat floats."

One winter, before I was born, it was so cold the lake froze solid for as far as one could see, and people walked all the way out to the Reef Light.

The lake lay below the city. Not far below, but just enough below that unless you were there, on the shore, or on one of its many piers, you were looking down at it. This we enjoyed doing, either from out our car windows, as we drove along the streets that bordered the lake, or looking down from the grassy knolls, or from the gazebo at North Beach, with its bathhouse and sandy expanse, that extended all the way to the zoo, a full mile away. Along that stretch of land, on the bluff above the lake, there were permanent benches, where the elderly and the thoughtful sat, in quiet, looking out over the shifting colors of the lake.

Sailboats, rowboats, tugs, coalboats and barges traveled the lake and the river. And on the piers, the early morning fishermen, who had obtained their bait from one of the many garages that lined the streets that led to the pier, where minnow and crab tanks were housed, with the craggy, unsmiling attendant, shuffling from house to garage at all hours, answering immediately the buzzer inside or outside the garage door, placed there for his customers.

Cooks' Shanty was the name of the whitewashed shed at the foot of North Pier. It was just big enough for Old Man Cook to turn around in once, with enough lateral space for perhaps two tiny steps both right and left. He sold minnows, candy bars, potato chips, and rented poles for $1.00 each, 90 cents of which was the deposit.

Some fished. Others swam. While many were content to sit above the water in silence on park benches, or drive silently along the streets and look out over the water as they drove. It was one lake, but it meant something different to everyone. And no one could say, really, what that was, for themselves or for anyone else.

It was the lake. It was there. And so were we.

UNCLE JACK

The stigma of tuberculosis—which was considered at the time to be a fatal disease—was so great that I had always believed Uncle Jack had been gassed in the war, and was therefore unable to work and had to live on his Army pension.

This was the family version of his illness.

We lived the length of our block apart. Ours was the second to last house on the west side of Superior Street, and Uncle Jack's the first house (behind the church, that belonged to State Street) on the east side of the street.

Uncle Jack was a bachelor. I believed he could not marry because of his illness. He stayed at home most of the day, and from the very beginning of my life he was as much a father to me as he was an uncle. Unlike my father, he was calm and patient, and I never once heard him holler or lose his temper.

Also, he didn't take me for granted.

My visits to his home meant as much to him as they did to me.

If I cut my finger open (as I did once, throwing bottles against a brick building on La Salle Street with Mikey Kaiserlian), I went straight to his home, to be bandaged and fed—usually a peanut butter and jelly sandwich. Or, if I stepped on a nail (as I did once), I would be carried to his home by Mikey's big brother, Hart. Again, food and sympathy.

In fact, I didn't have to hurt myself to receive his undivided attention.

To know that I had someone to turn to when I was hurt and in danger, was a great comfort and solace to me. It was much better than going home, where I would get loved, scolded and fed—because Uncle Jack left out the scolding part. And his love was always as free as his sandwiches.

"Ha, Tavit, it's you," he would say, opening wide his door. "Again you have hurt yourself, vy, vy, vy. Come in, come in."

Or we would sit on his back porch steps, overlooking his garden of cherry trees and growing vegetables. For as long as I could remember he lived on the second floor and rented the floor below.

The birds were always eating his cherries.

They must have been more than a common nuisance, because one day he went out and bought a beebee gun and began shooting at them. I should emphasize *at them*, because although he taught me how to shoot, as well, and gave me a turn at shooting *at* them, we never loosened a feather on a single bird that I can remember.

I think it was because he refused to leave his perch on the back porch, which was a good twenty yards away from the nearest tree.

Son a ba gun, birds," he would say. "Vhy they don't go bother Veber, his trees, ha?" Weber was his sour-faced next door neighbor. "Vhat so sweet about Uncle Jack's cherries, can you answer me that?"

I think he was proud that his trees attracted so many birds. I think he liked having his garden sung in all day long by creatures that could fly. It gave him something complain about.

He didn't like taking things sitting down.

Like all of the other Armenians I knew, he felt cheated by fate, and he believed he needed to do something about it.

In the old country, from the age of five, they began putting him on a mule to take food to the workers in the field.

One day, a branch of his family—the Kherdians of Kharpet—were passing along the road on which Uncle Jack was traveling with his mule. They were the first members of the family to take the Turkish threats seriously, and were fleeing for their lives. When they saw their young relative, they invited him along (by now he was ten years old) and, without giving it very much thought, he joined them.

He never saw Kharpet again. All of the members of his family, with the exception of his cousin, Yeghnar, were wiped out by the Turks.

He only told one story from that time: the story of how he took food to the workers in the field on his donkey. And then, having said that much, he would break down and cry like a baby.

I don't think he understood his regret. I don't think he understood his life. What man does.

After we had shot up a tube of bee-bees, we would go inside. "Time we eat something, ha?" he would say. Food was his great solace. He had starved for a good part of his life, and then, after the war, the hospitals, the flight to Cuba to rescue his cousin, he lived with his relatives on State Street, and because they were frugal to a fault, he never was given enough to eat.

He bought the house on Superior Street so he could cook his own meals, and nearly every summer evening he would cook shish-kebab, and eat it, either with peda bread, or with pilaf and an old country salad. Then he would walk to our home, and no sooner in the door he would announce, "Do you know what I made for myself this evening, ha!"

Using a toothpick once he pointed to the hands of his wall clock and taught me what time was and how it could be read on a dial.

In his Model-A Ford he took us to picnics and to the yearly *Madagh*, to Chicago to visit his cousin, married now with a family, and—best of all—to far off Thompsondale, where the fishing was so special. While we fished he and my parents would gather grape leaves for summer canning, so we could have *sarma* all winter long.

And then, when I was almost seven years old, he left for Detroit and returned home with a bride.

Holding my mother's hand, walking up the back

stairs of his home, I despised the woman I was about to meet, knowing that from this day on, I would be visiting my uncle only in the way we were about to visit him now.

MY FATHER

It wasn't until I had spent a summer in Greece—where I saw my father on every street corner—that I began to understand him. I had known all along that he belonged to another world and time, but despite my understanding, I judged him and the others by how well they fitted into the American milieu. A strange value system, perhaps, but as I look back on it now, how else could it have been.

My father was completely out of place.

Not only did he have a thick accent, he spoke English so poorly I could never believe anyone outside our family understood him. He couldn't write English, and he would often stop me at my play and insist that I walk with him to Farmers and Merchants Bank and co-sign his X.

It was for this reason that he was unable to continue as a chef.

He was an intuitive cook, whose every meal was a masterpiece.

He ended up working for J. I. Case as a sweeper.

Deprived of the only vocation he was meant to have, he turned his talents to shopping. He would spend all day Saturday buying the week's groceries, walking from store to store throughout the city, saving a penny here, a nickel there, the sum total being the weekly ransom on his lost pride.

Before he left for his shopping he would ask me—and later my sister, as well—what we would like to have for our Sunday dinner, for he always prepared the Sunday noon meal himself.

We never gave his request the dignity it deserved, nor the respect *he* deserved, partially because it was very difficult to get excited about a meal that was more than twenty-four hours away, and also because the choice was so narrow: *something* or chicken, and chicken was always luxury enough, especially the way he prepared it.

But Sunday was another matter.

The world was too much for my father. Life was too much for my father. And my mother was especially too much for my father. Young, attractive, sensible and civilized (by contrast she was a goddess of sensibility, reasonableness and strength), without even trying she drove him around the bend every Sunday afternoon, which was the one day of the week he spent entirely at home. Either she would volunteer to help him, or he would ask her for something he couldn't find—a pot, a missing condiment, for always the thing he wanted was not at hand, and whenever he needed something, he needed it *now!*

She wouldn't be in the kitchen five minutes before he would start chasing her around the table with a knife in his hand.

She couldn't just give him what he needed when he asked for it, she had also to point out that the kitchen was mess: for once again he had used every pot and pan in the house, and even the walls and windows would need a scrubbing once he was done, etc.

We shouldn't have taken any of this as seriously as we did, but we were children, and we did—we took it very seriously.

"Vy, you!" he would roar at my mother, and that was the signal for us to charge into the kitchen and start pleading for sanity and order.

We were so emotionally overwrought by the time the chasing and arguing had ended, that we ate our special Sunday meal in silence.

He never understood why we worried so much about everything. His temper was his built-in safety valve. He never carried a grudge, had no petty attitudes, and forgot all about the fight he was having the instant it ended. Dark storm clouds passed through his head, followed always by a radiant sun. His very illness was a purging—but since he didn't understand this about himself, it never did him any good.

Everything *happened* to him, and how much of it he actually experienced is hard to say. Probably very little. He was simply too sensitive for his own good, and once he was deprived of his vocation he lost whatever balance he might have been able to attain.

I used to dream of one day buying him a diner, because even as a child I could sense what he needed. My mother would laugh at my idea, and bring forth all the reasons—sensible and true, of course—why it was not possible. She was living with two poets, one a budding madman, the other full-fledged. She had no idea.

But in defending myself and my father, I have to say in fairness to my mother, that my father did not have it easy with men, either.

He understood service, which is a very big thing to understand, but he did not understand all that he needed to know about being serviceable.

He had a reasonable love of his countrymen and his church, and because he was well known as an expert cook, he would be asked to prepare the shish-kebab at the annual *Madagh*. He went at it with the same terror-inspiring intensity he went at everything else. He was faster, better, surer, and truer about the way he approached cooking than anyone else. But he could not get on with his own people. What Armenian man can?

Each Armenian is, unfortunately, a law unto himself. Each of us needs a great deal of space if we are to function at all, let alone efficiently. But while we demand a great deal of space for ourselves, this is just what we will not give others.

One day, while my father was marinating the kebabs, another Armenian man on the church committee suggested that it be done another way.

My father roared at the man. "Do you know who you are talking to? I am the chef. I will stick you in that cauldron over there and cook you with the *madagh*."

He never cooked for the Armenians again.

He used to say that General Antranik was too good for the Armenians. They didn't deserve a man of his stature. His nobility had been wasted on them.

General Antranik became my hero.

He started cooking for the Veterans of Foreign Wars. Because he knew about service, about cooking, about giving selflessly—requiring only gratitude and respect in return—he found with the VFW happiness at last. They gave him what the Armenians never would. They began calling him Mike, and bought him drinks and slapped him on the back—and gave him acres of space for his madness to play and grow tired in and rest. He was happier than he had ever been— probably since coming to America.

And then one day, while painting the recently acquired Veterans's building on Main Street, he slipped from the ladder, caught his ankle in one of the rungs, and pulverized his ankle bone. When it healed he was a cripple. His right foot, when he walked, splayed on the out-step, the way a door will when it has lost the pin in its bottom hinge.

Nevertheless, he never gave up his long, urgent walks, nor his shopping, and never once did I hear him utter a word of complaint or regret.

The accident had occurred in the late autumn, and that Christmas we began finding presents, secretly left in our entryway. Every day for about two weeks, there would be several new packages left at different times of the day and night. We never once saw who had left them. Nearly all of them were for me.

They gave him what no one else had been able to give him before. They were his family as no other family had ever been. Every time I pass their aging establishment on Main Street, I silently thank them, for myself and for my father.

ARMENIAN COFFEE HOUSES

All of the Armenian coffee houses in Racine had closed down by the time I was old enough to visit them as a man. I had wanted to be able to walk into one of them, sit down, and be served Turkish coffee on a tray, with cup and jezveh—as it had once been served to me in a cafe in Belgrade.

In Yugoslavia, the tray also contained a small dish with several lumps of sugar. This was how I imagined it would be, had the coffee houses of Racine survived long enough for me to experience them as a man.

But they had all disappeared.

The one that bordered the playground of Garfield School, on Milwaukee Avenue—old, gray and decrepit—had been razed, and when I returned home, after a year on the road and two in the Army, there was nothing there, where it once stood, just a gutted ruin beside Rognerud's former (now tightly boarded) gasoline station.

I had visited the ones on Douglas Avenue as a shoe shine boy, confused by the male loneliness and racial sorrow, that seemed to mix so easily and terribly with the cigarette smoke, the scattered newspapers and the hunched backgammon players.

The proprietor would often be standing in back, in his apron.

"Who's boy is it?" one of the men would ask, after we had entered.

And the one I stood before, who had motioned to

me for a shine, might say, "Speak! Are you Melkon's son?"

"Yes."

"He says he is Melkon's son."

"He is Melkon's son," the one spoken to would say—this time to the man standing next to him, who had, of course, already witnessed the exchange.

"You!" another old one would say to my companion, "are you not Vahan's son?"

"Yes."

"Your father knows your name, then."

"My name is Khatchik."

"Thank you! Khatchik Koroghlanian. I am not surprised."

"You see how enterprising they are," the owner would say at this point. "Although they are no more than children, they have begun to earn their own livings."

"Kah, what are you saying! It is money for candy they are making."

I would look up at the walls, embarrassed, and find that I was being stared at, first by General Antranik, and then by President Wilson, whose photos hung side by side on the wall, where they served to prop between them a miniature flag of the defunct Armenian nation.

The coffee houses were always good for a shine and a tip, for both me and Lotch. But when I went shoe shining with Howie Sell, I carefully avoided them because I was ashamed to have him see how sad my people had become, and how different I was sure they were from everybody else.

Many years later, when I had become the age of the coffee house Armenian men, I would sometimes visit the coffee houses in Fresno. Whenever one of my writer friends would visit me on their way through town, I would take them to the Armenian coffee house on Ventura Boulevard, just across from the red brick Armenian church, and only a block away from the Valley Bakery, owned by the Saghatelian family, who were friends of mine.

I would order coffee in Armenian. "Medium for me, if you please, sweet for my friend." By then the sugar was added in the kitchen, and backgammon had been replaced by gin rummy. When the waiter left us, I would point to the photo of General Antranik on the wall, and the other revolutionary figures, as well as the tapestry of Sayat Nova, the famous troubadour. The photos of Woodrow Wilson and Franklin Roosevelt had long disappeared, even though they had been the only national heroes of the Armenians in the American diaspora.

In the 60s ethnic was in, and my friends were envious of my heritage, and thought I was very lucky to have such exotic (they wouldn't have put it that way, of course) material to draw upon. They didn't know that what I had written about Armenian coffee houses was largely imaginary, based on what little I had remembered from childhood, and founded largely on stories that had been handed down.

THE STRANGER

What was it I wanted?

What was it that kept me from ever having the security that seemed the birthright of my American companions?

The farther out my life went the more I became aware of my origins, the complexities that drove me, the conditions of my life that seemed to give me no peace.

But then, little by little, I began to see that the life I had been given was the life I needed. I had to understand my life, not anyone else's, but I needed all the other lives, too—and all the other places, as well as the longing for my own place: the one I had left and the one I was seeking to find.

What was this place? Was it also myself?

I began to find my way, and my way was writing. Through words I was able to recapture images from the past, and I began to find an order in the chaos in which I had lived. My meaning grew, and in growing it began to reveal the meaning of my life on earth.

It had happened in mystery, the mystery of words, the mystery of breath, and the mystery of the earth and the many roots we had placed there.

I had found a way, my own way, to persist.

(PHOTO BY: GUY HOFFMAN)

DAVID KHERDIAN